Art at

By Sally Cowan

Contents

More Art Classes!

I believe we should have more art classes at school. In my presentation today, I will explain why art is important for children of all ages.

Fun

First of all, art is fun.

Imagination

Second, art lets children use their imagination.

Skills

Third, art can even help children develop skills for playing sport.

Most children love to paint and draw. Young children, especially, like the feeling of paint on their hands. They like to draw with pencils and crayons, too.

As children get older, many enjoy using other materials, such as clay, fabric, cardboard and wool. It is fun to discover different ways to make art.

Children also love to use their imagination. Art classes give them the chance to be creative. They often think of different ways to express themselves about the same topic.

Art gives everyone the freedom to explore their own ideas. For example, these artworks are about pollution and the environment.

This artwork, showing a plane flying above a polluted landscape, was made with a computer.

A student made this collage to show how animals and plants struggle to survive in an urban setting.

When children paint and draw, they have to control the movement of their arms and hands. Art activities, such as moulding clay, strengthen the muscles in their arms, wrists and fingers.

Strong muscles can help children play sports. Children with strong hand and arm muscles have better control of their movements when throwing and catching balls.

I think it is very important for children to use their imagination, develop new skills and enjoy themselves at school.

More art classes will help make our school a great place to learn.

Review of the week

The Friendship Art Display

By Effie Caridas, Year 6

The Friendship Art Display is taking place in the school hall this week. The artworks have been created by students from the senior classes.

The senior class creating artworks for the Friendship Art Display.

During their art lessons, Mrs Jacobs asked the students to think about the topic of "Friendship". They could use any materials to make their artwork. The result is an interesting display with a wide range of styles and materials.

The vivid colours of the drawings are impressive. There is a beautiful drawing of two friends on a rainbow. Jade, who drew the picture, put this note under it:

My friend Zara and I are on a rainbow, which represents colour, light and happiness. That's what our friendship means to me.

An eye-catching painting by Noah of him and his dog, Shadow, reminds us that friendship isn't just about people. It can also include well-loved pets.

A collage of photos taken by Lita is simply called "Friends". The photos show Lita and her friends enjoying themselves. This artwork shows us that friendship makes our lives more interesting and exciting.

Finally, there's Henry's "Football Match with Friends". Henry made some colourful clay models of a group of his friends enjoying a game of football.

These are just a few examples of the work by some of the talented artists at our school.

I believe all students and parents should come along and enjoy our Friendship Art Display.